King Without A Crown

Afu Okosun

Afu Okosun.,
A King Without A Crown
Edited by: Jenna Cabbell
Published by: Afu Okosun
10 9 8 7 6 5 4 3 2 1

Printed in the United States of America

Note: This book is intended only as an informative guide for those wishing to improve their lives. Readers are advised to consult a professional relationship/life coach or counselor before making any changes in their love life. The reader assumes all responsibility for the consequences of any actions taken based on the information presented in this book. The information in this book is based on the author's research and experience. Every attempt has been made to ensure that the information is accurate; however, the author cannot accept liability for any errors that may exist. The facts and theories on the issues presented are subject to interpretation, and the conclusions and recommendations may not agree with other interpretations.

Dedication

This book is dedicated to my grandfather, Stephen Nteff. May the legacy you left in the lives of others be felt and seen through me.

"I want to grow. I want to be better. You grow. We all grow. We're made to grow. You either evolve or you disappear."

- Tupac Shakur

Preface

"Nothin' ever comes to those who just wait,
don't ever lose sight of your goals; just keep straight."

Before I sat down to write this, I wondered, pondered and imagined my first words. Would I have writer's block? Would my otherwise thought-filled, opinionated head be left completely barren? Well, it isn't...and I'm actually doing this shit.

You know how everybody you know says the same thing? "Man, I should write a damn book!" How many people do you know who actually do it? I don't know any. People's lives are filled with stories they can tell; some amusing, some boring as thee fuck. What makes a good book? A good story? What makes someone worth listening to and what they say or write more credible than another? Is it a PhD? Is it the " _____ (fill in the blank) expert" title? What made Martin Luther King's words more profound than Joe

McDonald's, the pastor from down the street who preached the exact same message?

The difference, to me, is that they *did* it. They stopped talking about what they wanted to do, the "what if," the "should'a-could'a-woulda's" and actually did what they said they would. They stepped out on faith, unyielding and unaffected by the criticism of the world and just *did* it. This is me doin' it, like LL Cool J said.

This book is not an autobiography. Trust me, you don't want to read 200-300 pages about my life. Hell, I haven't done shit...YET! I'm just a young nigga hustlin'! This is a book full of my thoughts and opinions on a variety of issues. And please excuse the back and forth from slang, Ebonics and Twitter lingo to the "King's English," like my mama would say. I just want you to hear these words as you read them. You see, I am a very opinionated young man. A black man. One who God has allowed to see quite a few things in my 22 years on this Earth. Because of this, I have been able to positively affect those around me with my words of advice, encouragement and what I would like to think of as wisdom. Now while I have been an avid user of social networking to do this (follow me @FoomBoom,) I feel that there is much more that I am called to do.

Once again, this book is not an autobiography. But what I will do in this book, unlike many other books about the intricacies of human relationships, is relate my message to my own experiences. The one thing that I've always had a problem with when reading or skimming through books, statuses and advice on relationships and people in general, is that the authors never reveal enough about themselves. They may include a few scenarios in their lives that are played out in a point that they are trying to prove, but that's about it. It leads me to ask myself, "What makes you such an expert on this? For all I know, you could be full of shit!" How do I know if what these writers are writing is based on personal experience or if it's just a matter of accepted ideals or a reflection of what they have seen in society? This is why I'm doing this.

Everybody has an opinion and something to say. But so often, bullshit becomes credible information and we as people lack the ability to discern what is real from fake. Nevertheless, we still read the books and we buy into the message. I've come to realize that the things that keep people going are their relationships and how they perceive these relationships. Whether they are parent-child, husband-wife, boy-friend-girlfriend, teacher-student, etc., this is what makes us work. So, we are receptive to this surplus of information and relationship advice.

As I write this book, I sit here in my apartment in Huntsville, Alabama, seven months removed from my college graduation. I work part-time at a sporting goods store, and don't ask me how I'm making it from month to month because only God knows. This time of my life has been filled with the highest of highs and the lowest of lows. Why am I writing this book? To be honest, mainly for my sanity. So many thoughts run through my head on a daily basis that it would be a sin and a travesty for me not to share. What is wisdom if it is not shared? *Knowledge with no purpose?* With this conviction, I am driven to write this and it **will** be published. Sometimes you have to speak things into existence to see them manifest.

I'm writing this book for every young "nigga" who hasn't found his niche in society yet but is filled with that scary ass word: potential. For the niggas stuck "in between." For those who struggle with knowing better, and are actually doing it. For the ones faking it until they make it. I'm writing this book for the teenagers and 20-somethings that haven't quite gotten a hold on this thing called life. This is for those who just want to be better, have better and do better but don't quite know how to accomplish this without compromising their personal beliefs. This is not a success story, a how-to-do, 10-step, or act like this, think like that. It's just me, revealing myself to you and letting you know how I feel. This is me being transparent and allowing you in to know my insecurities, fears and emotions. I feel that if more people were like open books and viewed their lives as such, the walls that we build to protect ourselves and our insecurities would come crashing down. Own up and be proud of who you are, your life, successes and failures, because they are yours and make you who you are.

King Without a Crown. This statement means a lot to me. I don't know what Big KRIT meant when he made the hook, but I look at myself as such. I am a king, but who can tell? Where are my crown, cars, clothes and hoes? Why couldn't I have been born with a silver spoon in my mouth and be a self-proclaimed "real nigga?"

Who am I to tell you how to feel, what to think or what moves to make? This is nothing but my humble opinion. I'm just "talkin' my shit." As usual. Only this time, you will have a clear understanding of why I do it. And for those of you that know me, you better tell these folks that they may want to pay attention.

Contents

1
African Booty Scratcher

*"I wish I was a kid again, playin' wit my friends again
runnin' down the street..."*

My full name is Afumbom Songkang Osarieme Okosun.
Everybody just calls me Afu, Fu or any other variation of
Fu-something's they can come up with. I was brought
into this world on a hot summer afternoon on August 19,
1988 in Georgia Baptist Memorial Hospital in Atlanta,
Georgia to Misi Grace Nteff and Edobor Okosun. Yeah,
everybody from Atlanta is NOT a Grady baby (thank
God.)

My mother is from Cameroon, West Africa. Most
people look at me with the O_o face when I tell them
where she is from, until I say, "It's right next to Nigeria." Ohhhhh okay!

My mama came to this country in the early 70's
through Baptist missionaries from Iowa who became
her surrogate parents. Grandma and Uncle Bob. There,

my mother went to nursing school and was the only black student to graduate in her class. Now my mama wasn't the first of my family to come to this country; my Aunt Hannah was the trailblazer. She came first, with her main priority being to get her education and bring her siblings to this country.

Their father, my grandfather, Stephen Nteff, was a Baptist preacher. In addition to my mother, he fathered five other children, five daughters and one son with my grandmother, Maria Nteff. I always wondered why they had "regular names" and I got stuck with the Kunte Kinte moniker??? Sorry, I digress. Now with the exception of his popularity as a people's person and his calling to preach the Word of God, my grandfather's riches were few and far between. I never had the opportunity to become acquainted with my grandfather, but from what I've been told, he was a great man and a non-traditional African man at that time. While the culture expected women to take a back seat to men in many ways, he instilled a confidence and a work ethic in my mother and aunts that rivaled and surpassed many of their male counterparts. Needless to say, all of my aunts have earned college degrees. My grandfather's main focus at that time was to see his children get their education and make better lives for themselves. My mama told me he would always say, "First is your God, then your family, then your education."

I was raised on the south side of Atlanta. We lived in College Park until I was nine years old and then we moved right around the corner to Jonesboro/Riverdale. Growing up, my world consisted of 3 things: me, my mama and my little brother, Ehi. We were a team. My mother and I, alone by ourselves, were a completely different dynamic. We were, and still remain, partners. When I was young, our situation forced me to grow up a lot quicker than most kids. My mother was a single mom working full-time with two children who had to be raised. My father, at the time, was really non-existent. He was more like a shadow in our lives than a real figure. He was just the mean man who stayed down the street who would come by and beat our ass every now and then whenever we got out of line....or whenever he got hungry and coerced my mother into cooking for him.

At the time, we were living in Summertree Condominiums. It wasn't the best neighborhood on Bethsaida Road. My mother worked two jobs and was often forced to leave me at home to watch over my little brother. This was the life we had to live, and this was the partnership that we shared.

I never complained; my mother did the best that she could. She was and still is my hero. Most people work to take care of themselves and their children. She worked to take care of us simultaneously sent money "back home." My childhood was filled with conversations between my mama and her siblings about what was going on "back home" and what they needed to do to help. I think this is where I get my sense of selflessness. See in our culture, the family unit is larger than just one man, his wife and his children. Nephews, cousins, second cousins, aunts and uncles are regarded as brothers, sisters and surrogate parents. The depth and devotion that my mom uses in speaking about my cousins, one would think she is talking about her own daughters. This is a culture where it is expected to give and help without thinking, knowing and accepting that "borrowed" money will never be paid back. Without this selfless giving, my family would not have made it to America. It is this selfless giving that raised us as a people to higher levels. And it is this selfless giving that is becoming non-existent today.

It was seeing my mother work as hard as she did my entire life that subconsciously created a mindset in me. Truth be told, my mother is probably the smartest person I know. She just recently completed her doctorate in nursing. Yes, my mother is a doctor. It is very commonplace for me to be out all night, return home at three o'clock in the morning and walk in the house to see my mama wide awake at her desk studying or doing some kind of work. The crazy thing about it is that her earning power never really occurred to me until now. She nearly has the entire alphabet behind her name: R.N., B.S.N., M.S.N., F.N.P, and now D.N.P. She could easily have been earning over $100,000 a year. However, for the past 20 or more years, she worked as an assistant professor at the local university. *Why?* Simply put, to raise us. This gave her the flexible hours she needed to prevent becoming an absent figure, like many of the parents of my peers. Her career choice gave her the flexibility to remain paramount in our lives so she could discipline us and raise us right.

When I was younger, it used to always frustrate me that I never had the good shit everybody else had. While my friends rocked Jordan's, I was forced to wear the Olajuwons. Oh yeah, Hakeem Olajuwan had his

5

own shoes, and yours truly had a pair. I will never forget those UGLY ASS SHOES. I never owned a Sega or Nintendo when they were 'in," and when everybody owned Playstations and Dreamcasts, I was just mastering the Nintendo 64, blowing air into cartridges just to make them play. Now don't feel sorry for me, because we weren't dirt poor and my mama made sure we were fed, clothed and had everything we needed...with "needed" being the key word. Christmases consisted of receiving an average of 2 or 3 gifts apiece from Mama with an assortment of clearance sweaters from JC Penney and miscellaneous clothing items from family members. My birthday consisted of a crisp 50- or 100-dollar bill that usually ended up going towards school clothes since my birthday is in August. All in all, she did what she could, and she did it well.

Now keep in mind, the young man that I am today is *not* the apprehensive, shy, self-conscious little boy from College Park. Paint this picture in your head with me: This is Atlanta, GA. In the mid-90's. Old National. Freaknik. Back when the Ritz 2 was Ingles, World Changers was still located in the Old Chapel instead of The Dome, and if you didn't play park ball at Old

National, Flat Shoals or Welcome All....you get my point.

I attended a Catholic School named St. Johns in Hapeville, GA all the way up until second grade. I know my readers may be saying to themselves, "WTF?! This nigga went to Catholic School! HA!" At this time in my life, my father was pretty much a nonexistent figure. But he was a nonexistent figure with GUAP. He had the finances. Hell, he's a pharmacist. He enrolled me in Catholic School, and I took my happy ass up to Hapeville for three years straight.

Now while growing up in College Park, I met who would be the person to change my life forever, Coach Juan Raines. His son, LaJuan, and I met when they moved into the neighborhood. LaJuan and I became best friends instantly. Coach Juan coached at Old National Park and he thought it would be a great idea if I came out and played for him. Now I was a "husky" little boy, so it didn't take long for him to convince my mama to let me play in order to "get in shape." Playing at Old National, and then Flat Shoals when we moved was an experience in itself. This was my introduction to the real College Park. Waking up early on Saturday mornings, going to the park and eating a breakfast full of grits, eggs, sausage and orange juice, going out and killing whichever team we had on the schedule, and then hanging out at the park all day and riding around Old National with my coaches seeing God knows what.

I thought my coaches were the coolest niggas in the world. Riding around in Acuras and old-school drops with the hydraulics built in them, smoking Black and Mild's. Coach Juan used to wear this Kangol that I thought was the coolest shit in the world. And then his wife, Ms. Tura, was the finest woman I had ever seen in my life, at the time. I was thinking, *Damn, is this how you're supposed to live?* I always had so much fun when I was with them and they accepted my young, African ass like my name was Tyriq and my mama was from the 4th ward. The Raines were like my other family, and still are to this very day.

You ever just feel out of place in life and no matter what you do, you never feel comfortable? Well that's what I experienced as a child. I went to Catholic school with all these kids who really had nothing in common with me, who came from wealthy, affluent families while I lived in a condominium with my mama, little brother, aunt and mentally-ill cousin. And then I came home to my neighborhood full of African-American families who, in my opinion, were the epitome of cool, everything I was not. I was this chubby, black ass, little African boy named Afumbom, who owned two pair of jeans and wore Spaulding sneakers. I looked like an immigrant but was as "Collipark" as they came.

Because of this, I was very insecure as a kid. Everybody knows how kids can be some mean motherfuckers! The term "African booty scratcher" had a whole different meaning to me. I used to hate going to school when we had a substitute teacher for the day. Walking in class and seeing an unfamiliar face always brought chills to me. Why? The damn attendance roll. I dreaded those two minutes more than anything. Substitute teachers didn't know who was who, so of course, they had to call the roll. And unlike my teacher, who knew to just call me Afu, this fool was about to pronounce my whole name! I have one of the most African names that I have ever had the pleasure of reading. The name Afumbom comes from the Kom language in Cameroon and means "God's Gift." My grandfather, who said that I was God's gift to my mother, gave me the name. However, at eight years old, who gives a fuck about what their name means? To add insult to injury, Afumbom just sounds like I came straight off the boat.

Now it always killed me, and still does, how Americans can completely butcher a foreign name. It makes me wonder, "Don't you have a degree? It's called phonetics! SOUND IT OUT!" But it never failed, I would be sitting there dreading the initial pause, the confused "what the f is this" look, and several horrible attempts to try and get my name out of their mouths. Hearing the laughs and snickers from my classmates always made me feel this big ><. Hell, after a while, I would memorize the roll order and yell out "HERE!" before they even had a chance to murder my name. I promise, it took me until my junior year of college before I got over this shit.

I was like a fish out of water. I never really knew who I was or what I was. When I said I was American, they said, "No you're not, your parents are from Africa, so you're an African." When I said I was African, they said, "Um, no you're not, you were born in Atlanta, you're an African-American." My skin color didn't make it any easier. Let's just say, being black as hell in the early 90's was NOT "in" just yet. Sometimes I would catch myself asking God, why couldn't I just be "regular" like everybody else? Why couldn't my family just be "regular black" and not *African* black? (This was the conversation of an 8-year-old to God)

Now take all of these things I just told you, roll them up into one big, melting pot of poverty and emotion and there you have ME. This was me in a nutshell as a child; one confused little black boy wondering why and what it was that God had for me. So given all of this information, it would be pretty safe to conclude that I was a pretty emotionally unstable. And we have yet to throw in the wild card. My daddy.

2
Something

"*Something's…got a hold on me…something…*
is bothering me…"

My father's name is Edobor Maurice Okosun. This is
the one thing that I know about him without a shadow
of a doubt. Everything else that I tell you all can be
taken with a grain of salt because this is all that I can
remember being told. He is from Nigeria, and no, he is
not Ibo or Yoruba. He's from another tribe close to
Benin. I get extremely emotional as I write this and I
will try my best not to include details that are too
degrading in nature. My mama always says that
regardless of anything that my father has done to me,
he is STILL my father. Yes, technically, he is.

What little I do know about my dad is that he was
an athlete. He came to this country playing tennis and
from what I've heard, he was pretty damn good. I

honestly can't remember which institute he attended for undergraduate school, but I think it was somewhere in Jacksonville, Florida. He graduated from pharmacology school and became a pharmacist. Dr. Okosun. Yep, that's my father. Now take a young, single man in his 30's, a doctor with his own pharmacy, living in Atlanta in the 80's…what do you have? *A motherfuckin' playa.* My pops was the man; he was a ladies' man. I can remember being a little boy hanging out with him, and I had several "aunties" that would frequent his house for "bible study." This nigga was as smooth as they came.

My mama told me that she and my father met while he was doing a lecture at Morris Brown University. She said she was captivated by his suave demeanor and his intellect. So, you see where I get it from right? At the time, he already had one child, my older sister, Synteria, but he was "single." He courted my mother and they dated for a while. To this day, I wonder what my dad did to my mother to get her "sprung" like I know she was. Keep in mind that my mother and father were never married. They had both my little brother and me out of wedlock and as many transgressions as my father committed against her,

14

she remains a loving, Christian woman and has never lashed out at him. My mother is one of the most unemotional, unaffectionate people that I know. If I kiss and love on her too much, she starts to push me off. It's funny to think of her actually dating because after my father, she never "dated" again. Every holiday that I can remember, my mama would always make two of everything. We would have two turkeys, two potato salads, and two dressings. All this for a man who left her high and dry.

Now to fully understand my father, I have to paint a picture. Imagine a General in an army of four. He was the General, and we were his soldiers. With my father, it was either his way or no way; there was no in-between. He was a stone-cold African man who liked to have things a certain way and that was that. I thank God almost every day that he and my mama were never married because if they were, I wouldn't be half of the man that I am now and am growing to be. In the early 90's, my dad was like a shadow to us; he was in and out of our lives on a daily basis. His being in and out was one thing, but the fact that he lived ten minutes away made that fact that much more ludicrous. We lived on Bethsaida Road off of Old

National Highway until I was nine years old. This man lived ten minutes away off of Highway 138 in Riverdale! Now if you're from the Southside of Atlanta, you know exactly how close this is in proximity. My memories of my childhood with my father are scattered with times when I would stay at his condo, which was laid out in luxury, if I must say, stuck in my room watching Bebe's Kids or him coming by our house to shell out beatings and my praying he wouldn't stay for dinner, which he always did. It took time and growth on my part for me to finally realize the extent of his bullshit.

As mentioned previously, when I was younger, my pops had that "bread." As a pharmacist with his own pharmacy downtown, he was living pretty damn well. He had this black Volvo that, at that time, was almost like having an Acura or a BMW. It had tan leather seats and all these buttons and gadgets that made me view him as "the man." His condo was another world altogether; all white, plush leather sofas, artwork on the walls, big screen televisions, he had it all. My father enjoyed, no, he *enjoys*, the finer things in life, and that's something he's passed on to me as well. He lived in the condo with his brother, my uncle Eron, who at the time was a part-time body-builder and limousine driver. So, you can just imagine the amount of fuckery that went on in that house. They were two single men in their early 20's and 30's in the early 90's; needless to say, they "got it in."

As I grew older and we moved to Jonesboro, I stopped attending private school. To this day, I don't know why I stopped going, but I'm sure it was because my pops wasn't interested in investing in my education any further. We were moving on up because we moved into a house in a suburban neighborhood that, at the time, had a diverse mix of people and was not poverty-ridden. This was the time that marks the beginning of a real change with my pops. He was already a shadow to us, but at this point, he became a broke, shadow. He gave up his pharmacy downtown, his home was foreclosed, his vehicle repossessed and he essentially quit working. So here was a doctor who was living in a homeless shelter. *Hard to fathom, right?* Well, believe it. And this was his explanation: He felt that "God" told him to not work anymore and that he had to listen. *Crickets* *So God, maker of Heaven and Earth, told him to stop working, live in a homeless shelter, take care of his responsibilities even less than he already was, and totally*

disregard being a man? The situation grew so serious that
he even moved in with us for a year. One whole year.
That was probably the hardest and most miserable year
I've ever had to endure in my life. It consisted of eating
runny eggs and Raisin Bran every Saturday morning
and not being able to do anything unless "The General"
said so. I used to wish my mama would just kick him
out but I knew that would never happen. The simple
fact that he was our father was all the reason she
needed to take care of him and make sure he was
alright. God bless my mama, because if it would have
come down to my decision, his ass would've been
living in that damn shelter.

After leaving our house, my dad became scarce for
a few years, all of this within 10-15 minutes of our
house. He would bounce around from shelter to hotel
and from hotel to shelter. All I knew was that he was
alive. As far as what he was doing... I didn't know and
honestly could give a rat's ass. See, in order to understand the animosity that I felt, or feel, against my father,
you have to view him from my point of view. He was
the father to me and my younger brother, Ehi. We share
the same mother and same father. To give a bit of
insight into the type of child I was as a little boy, I was

the token child. I rarely ever got into trouble, I made straight A's in school because honestly, it was easy to me, and I was responsible and mature for my young age. Ehi, on the other hand, was something else. He is four years younger than me, and as a child, "trouble" was his middle name. I love him to death, but the little nigga was bad. He would inappropriately touch little girls, his teachers would call home about God knows what, and if lying was a job, his ass could have easily made 6 figures. So with this being the household dynamic, you can see the root of the majority of my mama's stress. What made my ill feelings for my father really take off was the fact that he showed favoritism to my brother. Even at a young age, I could tell that he spent more time trying to connect with Ehi than with me. Every time he called the house and I'd answer, he would never talk to me or ask me anything. The first thing that would come out of his mouth was, "Hi Afu. Where is your mom?" or "Let me speak to your brother." To this day, my father has picked up the phone just to call and see how I was doing only one time in my 22 years of living. This fact became even more evident as I got older.

Getting involved in football as a young boy made it a staple in my life. It was all I had begun to know, and it was a major part of who I was growing to be. Since I was a tad on the husky side, as previously mentioned, my mother's whole purpose of encouraging me to play football was simply for me to stay in shape. She never meant for it to be anything more than a childhood sport. Clearly, my involvement in football exceeded her intentions and expectations. When I was moving from elementary school to middle school, the issue of me playing football in middle school came up. Honestly, my mother did not want me to play at all. Being a nurse, she was bothered by the physicality of the sport and all the possibilities of injury that could occur; to her, it made more sense for me not to play and just focus on school. I told her that she must be crazy if she thought that I was not going to play football anymore (I didn't say it exactly like that, but you feel me.) She knew that there was no way she could really stop me from playing, especially if I maintained good grades. So out of desperation, she took the issue to my father. Wrong move. My dad, in his General-like fashion, told me that I wasn't going to play anymore and that that was it. No more discussion. My mama knew she had made a mistake as soon as she consulted him. Who did this nigga think he was?! *You're going to tell me, a son that you barely know, one who has been the man of the house from the day I was born, what to do?! You done lost your mother $*#&$^* mind!!!* I told my mama that I was playing no matter what he said and I didn't care whether he agreed to it or not. He wasn't in my life anyway, so his opinion really did not matter as far as I was concerned. She knew that I was adamant about playing, so she dropped the issue as long as my grades remained up to par which, to me, was a given.

Now this football issue became the catalyst for what would be the constant battle between my father and me. He knew that I was playing and there was nothing that he could do about it. This was a man who thrived on control, so not being able to control this aspect of my life ate him alive, I'm sure. I had intentionally and purposefully disobeyed him and basically told him to go fuck off. So one can imagine his feelings towards me; pretty much non-existent. The feelings that I already had toward him increased ten times over. During my middle school years and by the time that I was entering high school, he had gotten back on his feet. He and my mother had an "agreement" regarding child support and he would give her a couple hundred dollars every month for my brother and me, which was the most he had ever done. But everybody knows how that c-support is; the only time you ever really saw it was for school clothes and holidays, if that. Now his antics to avoid me seemed to grow even more now. I think he felt like I was the one who got away, like he messed up with me because I was too strong-headed and opinionated (like him) and wouldn't ask how high when he said jump. So while my prowess in football began to grow and my academic endeavors thrived, his attention, although mostly negative, still remained on my younger brother. So as a 14- or 15-year-old, I'm asking myself, "What is it?" You couldn't have a better son than me; I was smart, athletic, and responsible as hell. *Why did I feel like the black sheep? Why didn't he love me like he did my brother?*

My father's indiscretion toward me was never so evident than in what I am about to reveal. This is one of two father-related events that have affected me the most. I'm going back and forth from different times in my childhood but it is necessary to provide a clear glimpse of what events have contributed to my becoming the man I am today.

In the sixth grade, I attended Pointe South Middle School in Riverdale, GA. I was growing into myself a little bit and somehow I began to run with "the cool kids," so things were looking up for me. Now one day, I was leaving school and headed toward the bus as I usually did. This was after football season, those in-between months with no practice because I was never much of a baseball player, so I went straight home after school. Today was different though. While leaving school, I was met by my mother in the front of the school. Now, my mama was never one of those "active" parents. She didn't go to PTA meetings, or join booster clubs because she was simply too busy and she knew I could handle myself. So for me to see her at my school, I knew something had to be going on. She greeted me and told me that we were going to meet my father. She never explained to me why we were going but she didn't have to; I was going wheth-er I wanted to or not.

We arrived at what appeared to be a clinic. Once we were inside, we went into a room where my father awaited. True indeed, this was a clinic. At this point, I had questions that I definitely needed to be answered. I'm not a hospital/clinic kind of guy, which is primarily why I didn't pursue the medical field in school, much to the chagrin of my parents. So, once I saw these nurses and realized we were there for something medically related, I was a bit concerned. Realizing this concern, my mama began to explain to me that my father had a genealogical trait for some disease and that they wanted to take my blood just to make sure that the trait had not been passed to me. This explanation was fine with me because I mean hell, he was from Nigeria, and I didn't want to inherit some Godforsaken disease! So, having my blood taken was all good with me. Before I knew it, it was all over and we were on our way.

Now fast-forward a year. A year older, a year wiser. One day, my mother and I were sitting in the kitchen conversing after we had just eaten. My mother and I always have these kinds of conversations, from back when I was a young boy up to today. Whenever I visit home, we always find time to talk about some issue of importance in either her or my life. Now this particular evening, we began to talk about my father. This was right in the midst of the issues that he and I were going through. He had just gotten off of the phone with my little brother, failing to say a word to me. I began to vent to my mother as I would some-times do. But this time was different. I was extremely emotional, almost like a volcano about to erupt. It just began to really anger me how he treated me. How could a father be this way to a son who does nothing but make everyone proud? I was the "family star," as my aunt put it. *Who wouldn't want me as a son?* My mother began to talk and console me as usual, stating that the rejected stone would soon be exalted and that my father would regret these actions in his old age. As I sat there and began to really ponder all of this, the day at the clinic popped in my mind out of nowhere. Why would this day come up in my head, considering that it had absolutely nothing to do with my thoughts at the time? Or so I thought. The more and more my mind began to process that day and the information that I had been given, one plus one, all of a sudden, didn't equal two anymore. Why would my parents all of a sudden decide to test me for a genealogical disease after all those years? Wouldn't that be some-thing they would have found out at birth? And why would they run a test like that at a clinic and not a hospital? At this time, I turned to my mother and asked, "That day at the clinic...that was a DNA test wasn't it?" She looked at me with fear in her eyes, knowing that the answer she was about to give me would eat my soul, and said, "Yes it was."

When I heard those words, my mind and heart instantly turned into Dale Earnhardt and started racing all over the place. *A DNA test? Really?* I mean, I knew that my father felt some type of way toward me because of my rebellion against him, but I thought that was the sole reason why he was so detached. I had no idea that this whole time, he questioned whether I was even his son or not. The first insulting part is that he was disrespecting my mama by saying she was sleeping around and, how I saw it, he was flat out calling her a hoe. Secondly, how dare he question if I was his son and not question Ehi?! I was furious! What did I have to do, to prove, in order for him to accept me? I had nothing. Right there at the dining room table, I just began to cry. I cried like a two-year-old child who had just gotten a spanking. This one took the cake. My mama did her best to console me, but she knew that these were tears that just had to be shed. Do you remember episode on The Fresh Prince of Bel Air when Will Smith's dad comes to visit and then fakes him and has to leave? Remember Will's reaction at the end? Priceless, right? That was me, almost verbatim. I was just a little boy who wanted his daddy to love him.

This was the first life-changing event in my father-son relationship with my dad. The second one came when I was a senior in high school.

In 2006, I was in my senior year at Mundy's Mill High School in Jonesboro, GA. Simply put, I was *that* nigga. My brother, Erroll, my other partners and I ran that school, and it was a beautiful ending to what had been the best four years of my life. I was a stellar athlete in football, had been offered scholarships by several Division 1 schools such as Marshall, Jacksonville State and Furman, but in the end, I chose to attend Alabama A&M University on a full athletic scholarship.

My graduation was a pretty big deal. My mama and Uncle Victor had planned a graduation party for Erroll and me. We were also going to have a joint party at Erroll's mama's house as well. Life was good for us at this time. We were "Hometown Heroes" because of athletics and were everybody's parent's favorite boys. Erroll and I were two determined young men because we knew that the only way we were going to go to college was on scholarship, and for us that was by way of football. Digressing a little, there was one more event that I could add to the list. On Signing Day (which is when all of the high school football players across the nation sign their letters of intent to play at given universities,) my family came and supported me at the celebration thrown by my school. My teammates and I stayed at school into the evening, signing our LOL's and taking pictures. My mother, brother, Uncles Victor and Albert were there, as well as my father. The main reason my father was there was simply because he too had to sign the paperwork. Don't forget that this is the man who never wanted me to play football and now I was receiving a scholarship from this same sport. One can only imagine how he was feeling at the time. He was being a good sport about the whole thing, all the way up to when he got ahold of my younger brother.

The program was winding down and we were all seated when he began his rant. He began talking to Ehi about football and how the sport wasn't for everybody and how he didn't have to play just because I did. He then began to say how he wanted him to just focus on school and go into medicine and basically planned his whole life in fifteen minutes. I recall sitting there listening to all this and thinking, *Really dude? You pick today of all days to come and rain on my parade and continue to put your focus on my younger brother?* This was becoming the story of our relationship. Nothing that I ever did was good enough. My mama told me not to sweat it, and I didn't. Fuck him. I refused to let him ruin my day. It helped when my little brother told me that he wasn't paying our father's antics any attention anyway. Needless to say, Ehi is going to Albany State University to play football. So much for that speech.

My graduation was being planned out and I was looking forward to it. Going to college and playing ball was the reason why we had worked so hard. We knew that the only way for us to get better and do better was to get a higher education, play football and let the chips fall where they may. Now in our culture, our family's culture at least, graduating from high school was really not a huge deal. It was expected. Coming from a family where all of my aunts and uncles had at LEAST a bachelor's degree, you can see why. But because I had done and accomplished so much, they were going to celebrate me, "The Star." Because my family in America is so tightknit, I pretty much knew everyone who would be attending the graduation. Everybody else was a plus. This list included: my mama, Ehi, Uncle Victor and his family, Uncle Albert and his family, Aunt Hannah and my cousin Malaika. This was who would be there without a shadow of a doubt. Since this was such an important event, I was certain that my father would be there. My mama thought that it would be nice of me to call and invite him personally. "Sure, mother! I would love to!" Can you sense the connotation of sarcasm?

I picked up the phone to call him and I was nervous, as I have always been every time I called my father. The phone rang several times, and I was close to hanging up when I heard his voice on the other end.

"Good evening daddy."

"Hey Afu. How you doin?"

"I'm doin good, I was just calling to tell you about my graduation…"

"Oh ok…"

"Yeah, it's this Saturday at Twelve Oaks Stadium at 6pm. Everybody's going to be there and I was just calling to let you know where it was."

"Ok. Well Afu, I'm actually scheduled to work out of town this Saturday...so I don't think I'm gonna be able to make it. Aren't you having a graduation party or something? I can come to that..."

"(Pause) Oh ok, that's cool. Yeah, me and Erroll are having one at his mama's house. It's gonna be on Sunday."

"Alright, well I'll be there for sure, okay?"

"Alright daddy, talk to you later."

"Alright Afu, Bye."

And that was it. Just like that, my father had turned down my invitation to my graduation. He had said it so calmly as if he was rejecting an offer to go see a movie or grab a bite to eat. This was my graduation! Of all the days that he had chosen to be absent from, he had chosen one of the most significant, defining moments of my life. I turned to look at my mother and the expression on her face was one of disbelief; she couldn't believe that he really said he wasn't coming. I turned and asked her, "Are you serious?! Really? My graduation?! Wow..." I was at a

Afu Okosun

loss for words once again because, in his fashion, this nigga had done the unthinkable as if it was nothing.

So at this point I was furious. Too mad. I was angry enough to punch a hole in a wall. My entire life has been an afterthought to him, and the one time that I ever asked him for his presence, I was denied! There was nothing you could tell me at this point. No words of consolation that could be given at this time because my father had just pissed me off to the highest level of "infuriation." He was all kinds of "fuck niggas" in my book right then and I was going to make it known that I was pissed off. First, I called my Uncle Eron, his younger brother. Now Uncle Eron and I were not that close, but he always played the cool uncle role, so I was going to use that to my advantage and vent. I called him and just pretty much let him have it. I went off on a tangent about my father that could have won an award in rhetoric. By the end of our conversation, Uncle Eron was simply agreeing with me and telling me to do what I felt necessary. I had told him that the next time my father and I were alone, I was going to give him a piece of my mind.

So graduation comes and goes. It was a great day for me because my family was there. My brother,

Erroll and I were preparing to have a great night. Hell, it was graduation night! So after a night full of fun, which will go un-commentated, Sunday arrived and it was time for our graduation party. Both Erroll and my family gathered at Erroll's mama's house and we invited our friends over for a good 'ole cookout and dinner. The day was going by quite smoothly. I was there with my girlfriend at the time, along with all of our family and friends. All of a sudden, in came the General. My dad pulled up and pretty much took all the wind out of my sail. But handled it the way I typically reacted, by ignoring him. He went into the house and I acted as if I didn't see him until I went into the house. I gave him a brief "Hey Daddy…" and returned outside with my family and friends. As the sun started to set, I had to take my girlfriend back home. While I was dropping her off, I got a call from my Daddy asking me where I was because he was ready to leave. *Go figure.* I told him I'd be back at the house in five minutes.

This was probably the longest five minutes of my life. Why? Because I had made it up in my mind that I was about to tell my father how I really felt. Seventeen years of living and I had never had an honest conver-

33

sation with my father, never had a "heart-to-heart." I was about to go off to college, he was going to become even more insignificant of a figure in my life, and I honestly had nothing to lose, so there was no better time. It wasn't like he could whoop me. Hell, I was a 230-pound linebacker headed to play college ball at the D-1 level. He was 5'5 on a good day and all of 200 pounds, maybe. I would beat the dog shit out of his ass, a scene I had already painted on the walls inside my head. Oh, I was ready.

When I got back to the house, I saw that my daddy was already outside of the house talking to my mother and waiting on me to get there. So I parked, got out of the car and walked toward him with an eerie feeling that something was about to happen. We started to walk toward his car. He asked me where I went and about how I hadn't spoken to him since he had arrived, blah, blah, blah. He went on to say that he wished he could have attended the graduation but he had to work. At that point, his words were going in one ear and out of the other, but once he stopped talking for a split second, I took that chance to say what I had to say.

I interjected and told him that to be honest, throughout my entire life, I'd never asked him to support anything. Then I went on to mention how my Uncle Vic took the time to be there although he had a wife and kids. Now this must have struck a nerve with him because once I mentioned Uncle Vic, his eyes bucked, nose flared and I could see that IT WAS ABOUT TO GO DOWN. This is when my memory gets a little blurry. All I can remember is him saying something about my mother and about me being an accident and it was all she wrote. I completely lost my whole, entire mind. At that point, every curse word ever written came out of my mouth toward my father. I called him everything but a child of God. I don't know how we got separated but it took everything in me for me not to kill my father. He had broken the one cardinal rule. DON'T TALK BAD ABOUT MY MAMA. And then to have the nerve to say I was an accident and that she tricked him into having me?! This nigga was trying to get killed! Seventeen years worth of anger, resentment and frustration exploded out of me all at once. I was crying, spitting, cursing and yelling at the man who had caused me the most hurt I've ever felt in my life. Not a girlfriend, not my mama, not any failure or disappointment could equal the hurt I had felt from him and him alone. This was WAY overdue. It took for my mama and aunt to start crying, to beg my father to calm down and to take me and walk me around the block for my anger to sub-due. As a man, you can't have your mama crying AND you at the same time. So that instantly made me calm down. However, the whole time I was walking, I was cursing the ground that he stood on. And in a mother's true fashion, my mama let me. She knew that this was something that I needed to do. My father had wronged me too much, and it was unhealthy for me to hold all of that rage inside. I had never been that angry in my life and I pray to God that I never reach that level of fury again. But once again, my daddy had found a way to upstage me on my big day.

In the days following this incident, I received a boatload of phone calls; calls from family, friends of the family and even people who I didn't really know who just wanted to give me some advice or words of encouragement. Most of it, I took in, but there really wasn't much that could be said to me at the time. He was wrong. Point blank period. My mother did remind me, and I'm glad that she did, that no matter what he did, he was still my father. She reminded me that the Bible instructed me to honor thy father and thy mother so that my days will be long on the earth. She told me that even though he was the one at fault, I still needed to go to him and apologize for cursing him out. As much as I wanted to do the opposite, I knew deep down that my mama was right. Not even for him, but for myself, I needed to apologize to him. Because of what had happened, my Uncle Eron was trying to play mediator between my dad and me and had somehow orchestrated a sit down between the two of us. Long story short, I apologized for what I said and my father made a sorry attempt to try and apologize and rectify his actions in hopes of a better relationship. Once again, his words fell on deaf ears.

To this day, our relationship has never been the same. The resentment is still there but God is working on me. In true African fashion, he acts as if it never happened. As if everything is fine between the two of us. Not by a long shot. His words mean nothing to me now. And even as a teenager, I would rather see a sermon than hear one any day.

3

I'm Grown Shawty

"Time never waits for no man, peep the slow hand, lions is all, we rarely know lambs, get money, split it up wit my broham, when you go outside don't let the door slam..."

My childhood was interesting, but because this isn't an autobiography, I won't get into the intricacies of me and the specifics of how I was raised. My goal, rather, is to provide details and events that support the purpose of this writing. This chapter might be the most important one, simply because this one pretty much gives you the major reason why I am who I am and why I think how I do.

It is my opinion that a young man's life begins to be truly molded when he enters high school. I say this because it is in high school that he starts to develop a real sense of self and get a feeling for what he is and is not capable of doing. Middle school is one big bowl of questions. High school makes or breaks a lot of people, and I've come to find that high school is the peak of most people's "higher education." It is the last structured, controlled environment in one's life. It is almost a world in its own, filled with government (teachers and administration), hierarchy (the cool kids and the lames,) and what every community in this world has: drama.

High school is where I became Afu. I say that in the sense that, I was never myself until I got to high school and I began to see myself for who I truly was on the inside. You see my self-esteem was still a true work in progress when I left middle school.

I had been one of the "cool kids" and grew up around older kids who schooled me on everything from girls to guns. My mama never knew the extent to the things that I did at such an early age. You couldn't tell me that we weren't grown. I clicked up with a group of young niggas who pretty much ran shit.

This was in the 7th grade and we were 12 going on 20. The clique included the ringleader, Jamenski, a half-black, half-Puerto Rican hothead whose house was the "spot." Chris was the smooth, slick-talking one who was my road dawg. Ced was the Zone 1 transfer who was quick to swing on a nigga and take his bitch in the same day. This was how the clique started. It ended with a few more people but we were tight from jump. What made us so unique was that everybody played their part. My part, or so I thought at the time, was to be the cool, laid back one. I've always been a naturally reserved person and their personalities were enough that I didn't need to be outgoing. I could be me. But by being with them, I was introduced to things that I NEVER thought I would encounter. The most important thing that I did get from them was that as much as I was a part of the clique, I was that much different.

Middle school is where I was properly introduced to street shit. It was my 101 class. I learned how to talk to females, became a skilled rapper, learned how to shoot a pistol and roll a blunt, and most importantly, I learned the ins and outs of the female anatomy. I got this street education all while being in the gifted academic program as well as playing basketball and football. My life was so camouflaged because I had become a master of adaptation. I was able to adapt to the fact that although my clique may have been the school's worst, I was clearly one of the school's best.

41

My love for them had a limit, because although they were my friends, their lives could not be mine.

I understood this, and I maintained this role all during middle school. So although I had this "role" down pact, I still feigned to find the person who I truly was inside. I knew it was not in the shadows of the friends I had grown to love. But while middle school was my introduction to myself, high school became my perfection of myself.

I went from Pointe South to Mundy's Mill High School. It was a slightly different situation in the fact that this was a brand new high school. The surrounding high schools (Lovejoy, Riverdale and Jonesboro) were becoming overpopulated, so hence Mundy's Mill was brought into the equation.

So while most high schools went from 9th to 12th grade, we only had 9th and 10th. So I was a freshman at this new school, which at the time was nothing but a slew of trailers in the parking lot of Lovejoy High School. The actual school was still being built. Over the summer, I had been a regular at football workouts, but unfortunately, I never stood out. See I wasn't one of the "big" names that we had. Ironically, my two brothers, Darius and Erroll, who had been beasts at running back at Mundy's Mill and Kendrick Middle School's respectively, were the coach's favorites. We also had players like Levi, Mackie, Kerry and a few more upperclassmen who were above me on the totem pole.

While a lot of my peers passed the eye test, once those pads came on, it became a different story. What I lacked in physical features, I made up for in toughness, knowledge and ballerism. Yes, I made up a word, but that's what I was...A BALLER!

I became a starter at middle linebacker from day one and never gave up the position. I was one of the few "ballers" that were underclassmen, and by the time that my 10th grade season was complete, I was getting recognition as one of the best in the region.

Coming from Pointe South and from the group of friends that I had made while there, it made the transition to Mundy's Mill a little tough. I really couldn't kick it with them the way that I wanted to due to football. I saw myself slowly but surely losing touch with them. They were hotheads; a few of them got into fights and sent to other schools while a few just gave up school altogether. So for me, I was really trying to "get in where I fit in." My boys from the neighborhood were a year older and a year invested at Lovejoy High School, so they had made names for themselves already. I felt somewhat out of place in their company because their friends weren't mine.

Most of the players on the team came from Mundy's Mill or Lovejoy and if they did come from Pointe South, they were lames who I didn't associate with like that. But like the saying goes, "Birds of a feather flock together." Due to the fact that I was one of the better players on the team, and one of the more popular underclassmen, a special friendship began. In comes "my brothers."

Darius Woods and Erroll Wynn. Both were star running backs, both came from separate middle schools and each was "the man." What I've come to realize as I've gotten older is that although I hadn't seen myself in their same light, I really was on the same level. I was one of the best dressers in school, I was cool with damn near everybody, and I was a baller. It didn't take long before the three of us became friends.

It started out with football. Due to the fact that we were all young and in the same grade, it was easy for us to kick it because we messed with the same girls.

Darius and Erroll became close first and then somehow I was added into the equation. It's funny how we
all knew of each other in middle school and didn't like
each other to later becoming friends. Now, I've yet to
explain why I call these two "my brothers," but here it
goes.

From the time that the three of us got together, we
were pretty much inseparable. We were somewhat
similar to the dynamic in the film, "The Wood,"
except we were a southern, Atlanta version. Darius
was, and still is, the pretty boy, ladies' man. If women
were a major in college, he would have graduated
magna cum laude. I've seen him sweet talk the draw-
ers off a dyke, and I ain't talking about the ones you
watch on porn flicks. I'm talking about the ones who
have fades and rock Jordan's. Erroll is the rough one
out of the crew. And I don't mean rough in a literal
sense but just a little rough around the edges. Sometimes it seemed he didn't really think before he spoke,
but that was just him being him! And you couldn't tell
him anything either for the simple fact that he was
black as hell like me and everybody used to call him
Michael Vick. This nigga used to call himself "Black
Diamond" LOL. I always feel like God placed me in

their lives and them in mine for a reason. Where did I fit in? Well, I was just the cool one. Cool in every sense of the word in that I was cool-headed, cool mannered, and cool with the females. I was the solute to their solvent.

The reason why I stated that this time of my life was what really made me who I am is because I experienced so much during this period. Everything from my first love to my first orgy had taken place. High school gave us this nostalgic sense of self that, to this day, has never been duplicated. Going into my junior year, I was really beginning to come into myself.

At the age I am now, it's hard for me to really speak on high school relationships being credible because as we all have thought before, *who really knows anything in high school?* But even though I feel this way, I can honestly say that I experienced my first love in high school. Ariana. She was the person who has had one of the biggest impacts on my life when it involves to the issue of male-female relationships. For some reason only known to God himself, this half-black, half-Puerto Rican child protégé "chose" me when we were in the 9th grade. My first real suitor in my life, she let it be known that she wanted me and that she would have me whether I liked it or not. At the time, I liked her, but for the simple fact that I had options, I refused to go in completely.

So we dated. When I sit back and think about the conversations we had at 13 and 14 years old, they were definitely overage. She wasn't your average teenager and her talent at poetry afforded her the chance to experience things that most thirteen year olds could not. She in turn, showered this "knowledge" and love on me. At thirteen, I was still very much a work in progress, but I can say that she helped mold me and my thinking in such a way that I am able to think outside the norm today. Sad to say, at that time, the abstract person that she was in public didn't fit with the persona that I was creating. Her uniqueness and self-assuredness in who she was had not become a part of my psyche just yet. So with that said, after 2 years of dating, with one minor breakup and reconciliation, in the 10th grade we *really* broke up.

The breakup was ugly, even for a couple of 10th graders. When she came back to school that Monday, you would have thought that a family member had just died the way that she looked. It didn't help that we both took advanced classes together. It was so hard for me to look at her, knowing that I had caused this much hurt and pain. Why did I do it? Hell, I still don't know. But I think it was mostly because I couldn't take the pressure that she put on me. It wasn't by chance that she chose me. It was because that even at a young age, she recognized that there was something different about me. There was a man inside this young boy's physique that was ready to be groomed, molded and shaped into one that could love her.

But the nigga in me said, "Fuck all that. Where the hoes at?"

And from the time we broke up until my graduation, that's exactly what I did. Found the hoes. Yeah, I missed her and my insides yearned to be with her. But at sixteen years old, my insides, emotions and all that other mushy shit weren't at the top of my priority list at the time.

To put my high school experience in words is hard, mostly because I don't want to fill these pages with filth, but also because it was *that* much fun. To say that we did what we wanted was an understatement. From the classroom to the football field, we went hard. I remember days when I would go to school, only to leave at lunch to go to somebody's house where a full-fledged orgy would commence. Yeah, we had them hoes. From the 9th to 12th grade, our motto was, "If you're walking these halls, you can get it."

The crazy thing about it was, we did all this while maintaining "relationships." From our perspective at the time, "fucking off" wasn't a decision we made; it was just a way of life, almost like breathing. Whether you had a girlfriend or not at the end of the day, it was all about getting ass. As messed up as this may seem, it's the reality that we lived in, and still do. And this was at sixteen years old, so imagine how bad it could be now? You may think I'm over- exaggerating, but when you're raised how we were, you understand exactly what I mean.

The life of an athlete in high school consisted of two essential things: 1) Ball out so you can get a scholarship, and 2) Build your team. The first point is pretty self-explanatory. When you grow up with nothing but great athletes, continuing on to the next level is the goal at every step in life with the ultimate prize being to play professionally. That was everybody's way out and into a new life. And because every real baller got a scholarship, it was somewhat tradition. That meant we had to grind and ball to build a reputation as the best. And that is exactly what we did.

The second point may not be as clear. When I say "build your team," I'm referring to the number of females to which you had access. Whether you were just talking, going steady or only rendezvousing for sexual reasons, in high school, one had to have a team.

And I had one, so to speak, for the majority of 11th and 12th grade. Full of random females, some friends turned lovers and others acquaintances turned "fuck friends." The one constant I can say about high school is that we constantly were involved with the opposite sex. Football became a given, and for me, academics was never an issue, so that only left one thing. Growing up in the environment that I did, one full of self-uncertainty about who I was and never truly having high self-esteem, high school became my makeover so to speak. The things that had once been a negative in my life (i.e. my skin color, name, body) had now turned into positives for me. My dark skin color had now become an object of desire for females to where it once was one of ridicule. If I had a dollar for every time that I was told I looked like Omar Epps, I could help the debt crisis. I'm not going to lie; I started feeling myself a little bit. I wasn't one used to the attention that I had been getting. It was one thing to talk to females and be around them, but it was another to be the one they were crushing on or the one to whom they just wanted to "drop it off."

The pro-African name that I had once been ashamed of became my trademark. When I would make plays or big hits in games, all you would hear was, "FUUUUUU!!!!" I had an array of nicknames from Black Jesus, Midnight Blue and the most popular one till this day, FuFu. It was my African background and upbringing that made me different, and it was in high school that I began to understand this. It was where I embraced the fact that I wasn't just another nigga. I was truly an American born, African child who grew up experiencing the best of both black worlds.

Growing up "husky," my body had always been one of my biggest insecurities. Niggas always flex like they don't care about their bodies, but that's bullshit. We care. At least I know I did. Playing football became my saving grace as the older I got, the better my body began to look. But I was still insecure. I had, and still have, "man boobs." Laugh all you want, but I've come to the conclusion that no matter how big or muscular I get, they're not going anywhere! In high school, I began to accept my body for what it was and instead of focusing on what I didn't like, I worked on improving it every day.

So you can see that it was in high school that I experienced the most. I tell people to this day that my college experiences paled in comparison to high school. It's so crazy when I think of some of the reckless things we did back then because I know that I wouldn't dare do some of that stuff now. It just felt like things had fewer consequences back then, whereas now, they are life and death situations, literally. I thank God for allowing me to get out of so many of those situations unscathed, both mentally and physically. But while I matured and developed my self-esteem in high school, college was the place that humbled me.

In high school, I was a big fish in a small pond. Going to college, I became that small fish in a big ocean trying to fight my way back to the top of the totem pole. Along the way, I rediscovered myself, had some adversity, hard life lessons and ultimately began my journey to manhood. This college, Alabama A&M University, and my experiences while here have left an impact on my life in ways unimaginable. One that is seeing me travel down a road that I never knew existed for me. I've come to realize that the plans we create for ourselves, usually stay to ourselves never coming to fruition unless they're on God's agenda for your life.

My life may have not been much different than yours. I'm not naïve or conceited enough to think that my story is the only "print-worthy" story out there. But I do know that my story may resemble that of many young black men, and even women. The struggles that we go through on a daily basis on this path to self-identity and finding out who we are and why we're here have to be addressed or else we will forever be the generation that fucked it up.

They say that children are the future. Well I'm 23. The future is now. And I don't know where the hell I'm going.

4

Another N.I.G.G.E.R.

"...Waiting wit my hands out, broke in the hood they give a damn bout, bragging to my homies bout the hoes I fucked, drinking bottles after bottle cuz I smoke too much..."

When I go back and review the first three chapters, I almost want to go back and keep writing. See, my past has always and still does intrigue me. The things that I've experienced have molded me into the person that I am today and because I'm an ever-growing, ever-changing individual, I'm continually learning about myself. From my upbringing to my relationship with my father, my past is exactly like this book: Chapters in my life. They are the preface to the man that I will become.

But while I'm on this journey to self-discovery, I must address and discuss some issues that are dear to my heart. Issues that make me raise questions about our roles as young people, especially black men, in today's society. You see I AM a member of this "lost generation," and I feel that as a thriving and active member, I have the right to speak about us. I have the right to be a critic of sorts, to my people and my peers, because at the end of the day, I am only speaking about myself.

As I get in the car and ride to work in the morning, I put my phone on my New Shit playlist, put the shuffle on, and more than likely, you'll hear something from artists such as Lil Wayne, 2 Chainz, Drake, and Future. These are artists that I listen to. Mainstream artists whose subject matters range anywhere from sipping lean to learning how to love. Never would I begin to write that I don't love, vibe and ride to this music because that would be a bold-faced lie. I love music and although my friends know me to be a throwback, 90's R&B, slow groovin' music lover, I grew up in the south and hip-hop is what I know. Outkast, T.I., UGK, 3 6 Mafia, 8Ball & MJG, etc... you name it and I've been on it.

But as I sit back and think on the music that I listen to and the world that we live in, some things are slowly but surely becoming too commonplace. While artists have always been pioneers in fashion and cultural trends in society, nowadays these trends make me go *hmmm*. In the 90's, Tupac Shakur was one of, if not the biggest, rap stars in the world. His bold "I don't give a fuck" attitude and stance as a man took the world by storm. But when one takes a deeper look into Pac's life and goes past the Westside thug image and the "bust 'em up" persona, one will see a very unique individual.

Tupac studied at a school for the arts in Baltimore, Maryland. While there, he acted in numerous stage plays and was an avid writer of poetry. Interviews with Tupac Shakur were filled with intellectual conversations that were CNN and ABC newsworthy. What intrigues me so much about him is that he was so much more than what viewers and fans saw in the media. It is imperative to go much, much deeper than that to see the total picture. While Pac was a self-proclaimed gangster, he was also a man who knew who he was. While he rapped about fucking hoes and indulging in all the sins of the times, he also schooled us on the dangers of drugs, self-esteem of the black woman, and addressed the prevalent issues in the black community.

Today we talk so much about how "real" we are; everybody is or wants somebody who is "real." *But how REAL are we, honestly?* Men are looking for real women but only see little girls who don't know whether to be Beyoncé' or Nicki Minaj today. Women are looking for real men but only find boys whose identities change with every new Drake single. I hate this word so much because its definition, in my opinion, has become lost amongst my peers. My use of Tupac as an example was not only to point out that he was an individual who had a sense of self. It was also for one to see that while Tupac had a rock star persona and image, he ACKNOWLEDGED that he knew better. He acknowledged the fact that while he messed up and did a lot of the wrong things, there were issues going on in the world and in life that were bigger than the bullshit that we glorify and love. He rapped about his own personal struggle with knowing right from wrong and how his soul was torn between living the life he knew he should and the one he knew would lead him down the wrong path.

It is this personal, day-to-day struggle that we as a generation have completely disregarded. Instead of admitting and accepting the fact that as a people, we have problems and issues that we need to solve, we push them under the rug and indulge in things that mask the reality that is life. After reading about my relationship with my father, one can clearly see that I have a deep-seeded issue with the man. I'm no different than millions of young men who are fatherless or have problems with their sperm donors. But while I understand that this issue I have with my father is the cause of a lot of hurt and problems in my personal life, many of us act like these phenomena that plague us are not even there.

It is this "real" that I am trying to find. We get on social networks like Twitter and tweet about what constitutes a "real nigga," what makes you "lame" and what's the "cool" shit. The problem I have with a lot of these statements is that so much of it is completely superficial. "#realniggas don't drink Moscato" This is a real tweet that I read one day, and I thought to myself, *"Self, you must not be a real nigga because you drink Moscato!"* I like wine, whether it is red or white, and yes, I enjoy Moscato. There you have it. I'm not "real." Sorry. You see it is tweets like this that get re-tweeted and lead other young males to believe and feel that if they like anything that has a feminine connotation, they aren't worth a damn. Tupac was a G, but yet he went to a school for the arts, wrote poetry, was articulate, drank Alize` and to top it off....he had a nose ring! We would call him a "homo," "fag" or any derogatory gay reference we could think of nowadays. But the difference in men such as Tupac and us today is the self-confidence. Tupac knew who he was, what he liked and what he wouldn't go for, and he didn't give a damn what others thought about it. *Can we say this about ourselves?*

Honestly....*hell no.* We don't know what the hell we like. Let me use fashion as an example. Now we all know that fashion has its seasons and that fashion is really nothing but one big cycle with fads that come and go. All it takes is for an "expert" to say what's hot and what's not, and there you have it. And while music artists have been pioneers in setting fashion trends, it seems like it has been taken to a new level. Take hats for example. This time last year, you couldn't get a nigga to buy a hat that wasn't a fitted. Now, "snapbacks" are the only hats that come off the shelf. Why is this? It is the influence of artists such as Wiz Khalifa, who by themselves have started a completely new look for young black males. Snapback, tank top/white v-neck shirt, camouflage pants, and any new pair of sneakers. This is us. This is what we wear and what we constitute as being "clean." Walk around your neighborhood college campus if you think I'm lying. I bet all $115.63 in my bank account that this is what you will see.

Let me clarify that I'm not saying that this way of dressing is bad. Hell, I've worn this before and still do. Although I wear camouflage shorts for reasons other than fashion. My issue with this is that before Wiz donned the snapback or the camouflage shorts, we *never* even considered wearing them. We never thought about the fact that those shorts do go with damn near anything and that snapbacks never really looked that bad in the first place. Jerseys are the next to come back in style, all because my boy Wale never stopped wearing them. Because we lack our own personal senses of style, trends are not just trends to us. They *are* us. We have become trends, fads that change with the seasons. And it boils down to the fact that we lack strong senses of self. So again I ask...*What is "real?" Who are we?*

The baffling thing about this issue with self-identity, especially with young black males, is that the most lost seem to be the most educated, so to speak. Go to college campuses, especially HBCU's, and you find a huge amount of young men who don't know who they are. Why do I say this? Because most of us come to college with the notion that we have to reinvent ourselves, and in an environment full of scholars and intellectuals, we have to be the exact opposite of that. Thug : College . What would you do if you saw these words used on a standardized test in an analogy? Immediately, I would think, opposites. Thugs don't go to college, *right?* Well, tell some of us this because at my time as an undergraduate student, you would have thought some of these niggas grew up with Larry Hoover and Big Meech.

While we are expected to be the leaders in society, we shun from that responsibility and lean towards being the majority, not the minority. We embrace mediocrity because it's so much easier to be a regular nigga intellectually, but a standout in the superficial. It's easy to brag about what you have as opposed to what you know. Material things can be bought in seconds but knowledge has to be obtained over time, and because we live in a society that thrives off of instant gratification, you can guess which choices we make. There was a time in the world when young, black men were thought of as a force in the world and threatened white supremacy because we were intellectuals. There was also a time when young women wanted to be with men who had the most knowledge and not the most pairs of Jordan's. This not to imply that we don't want these things today, but the phrase, "Knowledge is Power" is slowly beginning to die in our community.

While many of the current books by Steve Harvey and Tyrese offer mind-blowing and insightful advice to the mystery that is the black man, one HUGE reason why relationship failures are increasing at an alarming rate is because of our identity crisis. We just don't know who we are anymore.

Brother Harvey said in his book that before a man can truly commit to a relationship with a woman, he has to be able to provide for himself and achieve a certain level of, what I perceived as, self-worth in the world. A man has to have reached a certain "status" in life before he can even think about entertaining relationship talk. What's interesting about this is that when I look at my peers and me, self-worth and status are the pieces of life that have extremely hard for us to attain.

The general consensus view of what a "man" should be has become questioned among our generation. I believe this is simply due to the fact that our role models and what we view as being successful have shifted. Very few young black men view success as the old "American Dream" with a good-paying job, wife and kids, nice house and a white picket fence. This is just not appealing to us anymore. *Why?* Turn to BET, VH1, MTV or any entertainment channel, and therein lies your answer.

In a time like no other, our culture and what we indulge in as entertainment is completely dictating what we want out of life. No longer do we aspire to be doctors, lawyers, engineers or any other industry that requires us to actually "work" to attain them. The dominating industry that we look to become a part of is the entertainment industry. When I log onto Facebook and Twitter, I lose count of how many rappers, singers, promoters, dancers and "teams" I see out there. From my graduating high school class alone, I know of several aspiring "musicians." O_o

And while there is real talent out there that needs to be discovered, some of us are really lying to ourselves. We look at the Drake's and hear the success stories of the Justin Bieber's and how they were "discovered" and instantly blew up, not realizing that these individuals have extreme, God-given talent. They were bound to be found. We watch programs on which the only successful people we see are athletes and those in the entertainment industry, with reality shows such as Basketball Wives, where exes and girlfriends of former athletes are able to gain fame from being associated to their current and former ball players.

Young men grow up nowadays with the idea that the only way to "blow up" or "make it out" is to: 1) play sports, 2) make music, 3) sell dope and eventually make your way to doing #2. This mentality is this way because we see too many success stories with this as the blueprint. Because we lack the real life role models and male figures in our lives to tell us otherwise, we take this and run with it. Now some of you may think I'm tripping or wondering why I'm being such an ass and on my "power to the people" trip right now but it's for just cause. Because up until a few months ago, this was me.

I grew up playing ball and playing ball took me through each phase of my adolescent life, from park ball to middle school, middle school to high school, and then high school to college. This constant progression for me was all with one goal in mind: make it to the NFL. Everything that I did was all with the idea that I would make it to the league. While I knew that the odds against me making it were extremely high, I always maintained my optimism. Hell, I was a baller. Who was to say that I wouldn't be the exception? Throughout my entire life, I had been labeled as "gifted." I had been in the gifted program, aced most standardized tests, and had scored a 26 and a 1210 on the ACT and SAT, respectively. I knew that if I had chosen to pursue academics full time, I would be the scholar that my parents truly wanted, but I wanted more. I have never seen myself as a 9-to-5, five days a week, working individual. Call me crazy, but this was never in my plans for my life. And while I'm finding out other ways to make this dream a reality, I had always perceived athletics as my ticket. God had given me a gift to play football as a linebacker. I had instincts and a knack for finding the football that made up for my lack of physical attributes. These talents led me to a pretty impressive college career. All-Conference selections as a junior and senior with 200+ career tackles and, if you ask me, one hell of a high-light tape. But with all of this said, my dreams of a career at the next level all began to die on my pro day.

On a day when NFL scouts show up and gather your info, make you run and jump and try to determine if you're athletic enough for the next level, I was scared out of my mind. *Why?* Because after four months of preparation, I had a hamstring strain that just wouldn't go away, so when it came down to running and jumping, I was definitely not 100%. While I knew that the scouts were really there to see my homeboy, former defensive tackle and current Carolina Panther Frank Kearse, I knew that this would be the only chance I had at being seen by NFL person-nel. So after the workout was over and I had done my best in every test, I began to face reality. The head scout had Frank and another teammate of mine do an individual workout and thanked us for our participa-tion. That was it. I've always been a dreamer, but I'm a realistic one. I knew what this meant. They were the only two players that they really cared to see and we were just there to fill space. I sat out there for a while, watching the scouts talk among each other and my coaches and was in a complete daze. It was if my whole playing career flashed before my eyes, because at that moment, I realized that this was the end. As much as I wanted to believe that I would continue training and continue to pursue football at the next level, deep down, I knew that it was over. My love affair with the game was at an end, and she had left me one bitter ass nigga. *Why?* Because I knew that all I needed was a chance. Well, my chance had come and gone.

I went into a sort of depression over the next few days as I tried to sort my life together. I was homeless, jobless, purposeless and emotionless. Or so I had thought. Football had really defined my entire life. While I had lied to myself that football wasn't all that I had and ensured that I had a plan B just in case it didn't work out, secretly it was all that I ever wanted. So now that it was gone, what was I to do? I was definitely at a crossroads.

Now this is my story (And more than likely the story of thousands of former college athletes.) While we played sports with the goal of attaining a degree, the majority of us played with the dream of a multi-million dollar contract at the next level. And it is these dreams of grandeur that plague a majority of the young men in this generation. Our definition of success only comes from fame gained in the entertainment industry. We no longer dream of being the father figure, head of the household that our ancestors envisioned us to be one day. To many of us, the idea of a monogamous relationship with a woman is so far-fetched that it isn't even ever considered. So, before we can begin to talk about the phenomena that are male/female relationships in today's day and age, we must address who we are as individuals first.

Because my father wasn't a huge part of my life, I can admit that I never learned certain things. This is not to assume that he could have even taught me, I would have had some sort of foundation with which to cross reference my experiences. If not for my Uncle Victor being in my life, I would have been even worse off. Things such as how to check oil, change a tire, cut grass, tie a tie, etc.; these were things that my Uncle Victor had to step in and teach me. But even today, there are certain "manly" projects and handy work that I feel uncomfortable doing. *Why?* Because I was never made to and never taught how. So while some of these books tell women to demand and expect a man to be a man, understand we are dealing with a generation of men in body, but boys in mind and spirit.

Experience is definitely the best teacher, but it isn't the only one. You don't have to get an STD before you realize you need to wear a condom. (Well some of us do...) If our fathers had stepped up and been the mentors and leaders that we needed them to be, who's to say where the state of black men in America would be today? What scares me the most is that while we are considered the "lost generation," we are making babies at an alarming rate. How bad off will our children be in this world? I'm afraid for our generation's children because we are nowhere near as selfless as our parents. So many of us are the products of single-parent homes, and we all have our own "Super-mama" stories. Our mothers slaved and sacrificed so that we could have. *Will we do the same?* If not, all you will be left with is a generational cycle that will continue to grow even worse if we don't step up and address the problem.

In Big K.R.I.T.'s song "Another N.I.G.G.E.R.," which this chapter is named after, he uses the word "nigger" as an acronym. It stands for Naïve Individual Glorifying Greed and Encouraging Racism. When one thinks about this acronym, it all too well fits what so many of us have become. While we have taken the word "nigger" and turned it into an endearing term, its core definition was that of an ignorant, incompetent individual (black) who was viewed as less than a person. One listen to the song and you can paint a picture of whatever hood you were raised in and see a few of your old partners out there on the SAME block, doing the SAME shit, day in and day out.

I've never been one to knock anyone's hustle. I'm a true believer in getting it "by any means necessary," but the problem we have is that we eliminate the different means we can use to get it by the decisions we make. The United States of America is such a wonderful country in that it affords individuals the opportunity to succeed no matter the state of the foundation. And while some of us have environmental factors that heavily influence our lives, there is still the opportunity there to be successful. We limit ourselves to only being artists, entertainers and athletes. The

71

God-given minds, talents and abilities that we have, we don't want to cultivate and grow into anything. *Why?* I feel that it is because we don't long to be true difference makers in the world; we only want the world's approval. Even those from strong households and backgrounds choose to succumb to the stereotype and instead of being a STAND OUT, we choose to just FALL IN with the crowd.

Read the JET and EBONY magazines and you may get a glimpse of some young, black, gifted individuals who are making a difference. So please believe that we are out here and we are doing things. My wish and prayer is that more of us follow suit and maximize our abilities as leaders in society, especially us young men. And while there many examples of successful black men in today's society, my question is, *"How did they get there?"* How many of us YGB's (Young, Gifted Blacks) have all of the talent in the world but no one there to lead us or guide us to where we need to go? Let's just pray that this cycle ends before another generation ends up becoming nothing but statistics.

5

Down & Out

"...if it's a white man's world, am I still a slave, to the
minimum wage..."

As the days go by, some better than others, one can't
help but sit and think about the future and what lies
ahead. It's crazy all that can transpire in one's life in
the course of twenty-three years, but what's even
crazier is all that has *not* happened.

Writing this book has been a vent of sorts for me,
and my way to get out some of the things that truly
and deeply bother me about my life, and society as a
whole. I started off with the idea that this would be a
book focused more towards intimate relationships
between males and females, but as I began to write, I
see that this isn't the case at all. I've read enough
relationship articles, books and commentary to write a
term paper. And while I'm very opinionated on the

73

subject, my contribution to that subject will focus on that which I can control and understand. Myself.

I'm a young, black man in America. Born and raised in the south. All I can do is speak on that which I know. I know how I was raised, I know my peers, and I damn sure know this culture. I know that as a young black man, the odds are against me at an alarming rate. My mama tells me every chance that she can, "Son, it's getting even more and more competitive out here. I'm just worried about you." Shit mama, I'm worried about my damn self.

Although I have a degree under my belt, I understand that that means all but nothing in today's economy. Unfortunately for me, upon entrance into college, I was unsure of the path in which to take because education was really just a given. I knew I would get a degree, but the reality that faces me now wasn't really even a thought back then. So I chose to pursue Community Planning and Urban Studies. A good field, although very specialized and concentrated, it appeared a good choice at the time. Four and a half years later, with a degree in tow, my number of options in the field are the about the same as the number of championship rings on Charles Barkley's fingers.

Looking back, I realize that I was ill-prepared for the future that has become my present- day situation. While my mother always warned me of the perils that I may face, the faith that I had put into the game of football surpassed it all. True indeed, I had many mountains to climb and obstacles against me, but as my life showed proof, if anyone could do it, I could. So, as I sit here now and fill these pages with my thoughts, one overwhelming thought supersedes them all right now. *WHY Y'ALL DIDN'T WARN A NIGGA?!* I mean, sure, my mama made it her point to let me know that things would be hard, especially in the field I had chosen. But I can sit here and honestly admit that I was not the least bit prepared for life after graduation.

Taking a look back at my time in undergrad, some more things begin to stick out to me. While I was a good student (3.1 GPA), my playing football prevented me from getting completed involved and thoroughly engrossed in the program. My professors knew that mentally, I was capable of greatness and I took it upon myself to show them that I wasn't just another dumb athlete who they had to spoon feed. But I can't help but remember that the times I did try and reach out to them for some sort of guidance, my efforts were typically unsuccessful. Don't get me wrong, some of them did offer advice, but none made it to the point where they developed a vested interest in me. For some reason, and I still feel this way to this day, my demeanor and the way I carry myself gives off the impression to people that I have it all together. Maybe they felt that I would be alright and that they didn't really need to help me out as much as other students. Boy, were they wrong.

As a student and as an athlete, I was striving to be the best that I could be, both in the classroom and on the field. Writing papers, doing projects, running sprints and making tackles; this was the life I knew. But it was the game of life where I need help. During my sophomore and junior years at A&M, this is when my true discourse and feelings about this situation arose.

It was right around the time that I had pledged Omega Psi Phi Fraternity Inc., and I was catching hell from my coaches. It was also a time in my life when, financially, I was on my own. Yes, I was enrolled under academic scholarship, but if you know anything about HBCU athletics, you know that money definitely doesn't grow on trees around here. Those of us on athletic scholarship would receive one check a semester for $150 and it would usually come late. A joke. So for me to go to summer school, and have a way to pay for a place to stay, I had to work on campus. Coaches would hassle me about "getting in extra work" and they sometimes said, "You're not working hard enough." I used to get so pissed off because all along I'm thinking, *"Motherfucker, you work a 30-hr a week job, take summer school classes AND make all the workouts and NOT be tired!"*

Now it wasn't sympathy that I was seeking, but I surely could have used a bit of empathy. They didn't have to feel sorry for me, but it would have helped to know that they understood that I was out there busting my ass! Times like these made me really question the character and integrity of some of my coaches as well as professors. Yes, I understood that these were jobs that they were paid to do. But when you hold young men's and women's futures in your hands, so to speak, one would think that you would do the best you could to make sure they were as successful as possible. And while many fill this role and do it well, the majority of my experiences were filled with more criticism than guidance.

So here I am. A year and a half removed from college and I'm just now getting "on my feet." Six months of homelessness, sleeping on fraternity brothers' couches, part-time and server jobs, all to stand on my own two as a man. This time has taught me some invaluable life lessons about myself as well as others. The irony about my situation is that I am, as we like to call it, "plugged up." In layman's terms, I know a WHOLE LOT of people; influential people, powerful people, CEO's and others who simply hold other people's careers in their hands. And I don't just *know* them; I have the privilege of calling many of them my friends. So imagine here I am going through a situation where most of the time I had twenty dollars to my name and living day to day, but at any given time, I'm rubbing shoulders with millionaires. From childhood friends who went on to play in the NFL to business owners who my friends and I worked with hosting social events, the irony in my life is crazy! My girl always tells me she has never seen somebody who is friends or acquaintances with as many rich people as I am. I think she gets even more frustrated than me because she knows that they can help me in some way shape or form. It is this reality, that they *can* help me, that has made my transition into adulthood that much more surreal. It has brought me to a place of reflection on my beliefs and faith because for a long time, I spent my days angry and upset that I never had any help. No, I wasn't looking for a handout; just a little push up the ladder. As we all know, it's not always about what you know, but who you know. And damn it, I know enough.

No longer am I as angry or bitter as I once was about my situation. My trust and faith in the God that I serve has awarded me the strength to curb my emotions and understand that everything happens according to His Will and perfect plan for my life. So, I'm coolin'. But I will say this; I do often wonder how many people are in a position to help change or better a young person's life but just choose not to do so. I've attended events by many organizations such as the 100 Black Men as well as my own beloved fraternity, and I am often surrounded by a plethora of older, established black men well in their 40's and 50's. Most are old enough to be my father, but my interactions with them are usually short-lived and full of rhetoric I'm used to hearing from an absent father. It's one thing to tell me what I need to do, but another thing altogether to show me. Our society is quick to point out the areas in which black men lack but fail to emphasize the fact that we lack efficient teachers. Mama did the best she could, but certain values and principles can only be properly instilled by the same sex. As a young boy, your mother can tell you all day how to treat women. But the older you get, your ideals become formed or influenced by your environment, and more times than not, this environment is full of people who look just like you. So like I said before, whenever I'm in these situations, I often find myself wondering. I've been told of my potential, praised for my character, given words of encouragement by the people who have watched me from afar. But all the while, here I am "tryna' make a dollar outta 15 cents." I too, want to have a family, wife and kids, and become the proverbial head of the household that I never had as a child. But in an age where traditional- ism clashes with reality, this dream is becoming harder and harder to attain. Degrees don't equate into jobs, education was once thought of as the way to ensure financial stability. Now it is seen as the surefire way to financial crises through education loans. But I digress. My point is that we need more coaches and fewer analysts; More men shooting in the gym with me rather than talking shit about why I can't make shots.

It's crazy how as a young, black man, there are timelines for our successes. The majority of mentoring programs and services I encounter are always aimed at the youth and children, as they should be. Children are impressionable and the influence they receive at a young age can shape who they are for life. But it seems to me that most of us by the age of 18, if we aren't on the right track, can easily be written off. Old habits may die hard, but they *can* die.

Point and case, one of my childhood friends who I mentioned in the previous chapters called me the other day. I hadn't spoken with him in a few months but I keep in touch with him through Facebook for the most part. So we started catching up on how each other is doing and then the conversation took an unexpected turn. He began to talk about his 2-year-old daughter and how he want the best for her. He's still at home with his mom and he starts to tell me how he just doesn't know what to do. He says he can't sell drugs out the same house as his daughter, and he's thought about going to school but he doesn't want to come off as "soft" to niggas in the hood. Yes, this is a real conversation. I tell him a little about my struggle, because most of my boys at the crib just think I've had it made, and start asking him what his interests are. The deeper we get into it, I begin to realize that he is completely lost. He has no direction, no foundation, and no one there to show him HOW or WHAT to do.

Conversations such as these are the ones that thousands of young men across the country are having on a regular basis. Not 8- and 9-year-old boys, but 23- and 24-year-old "men" who society deems as adults even though they are as lost as the children they father. How does one cope with the reality of a bleak situation without going to extreme measures to change it?

Go with what you know.

And that's exactly what we do. If all you know is the streets and you have no one there to show you otherwise, take our ass to the streets and make it "do what it do." The song says, "Hustle, Hustle, Hustle...HARD," but what happens when your hustle comes to an end? Who will be there to help direct you to a new path and a new "hustle?" The one thing that I've learned in this transition part of my life is that it really doesn't matter what cards you're dealt in this life, unless you have self-motivation, you can easily lose. Self-motivation is the one thing that no one can take from you because no matter the situation, it is the driving force telling you to reach higher heights and to do better. Without this, the innately great become good and the good become average and so on. But for MY PEOPLE, for the young, black men across the country that are just like me, I'm beginning to question whether it is a lack of motivation or just a lack of direction. See, a nigga will "grind" and do what it takes to reach his dream. But maybe the real issue is that these dreams are all beginning to look exactly the same. I'm not bullshitting; I swear all I hear and see is "check my new track out" and "field work" this and "free before 12" that. We have relegated ourselves to simply strive to become entertainers and/athletes. . Athletes **entertain**, musicians **entertain** and the misguided entrepreneurship that is party promotion is pretty much **entertainment**. And as a former athlete, I know how it feels to go broke for your dreams. I've endured the countless workouts, runs, film study, etc. that I knew it took to reach my "dream." My self-motivation to reach this dream is all that I needed to keep going. But guess what? I had to wake up. And when I did I saw that my dream was no longer feasible so I had to start back at square one...and find a new dream.

Yes, I was able to redirect my steps and set my sights on new goals but how many of my peers are struggling with this very issue? I'm betting that it is more than we think. We live in a society where negatives are displayed more than the positives. But as a college educated man, I have become fully aware of the amount of black professionals in an array of fields across the country. Of these professionals, that are men, I ask myself how many of these men take an active role or try reach out, maybe not as a group mentor, but to any young man who is not s blood relative. I wonder what would happen if these men took vested interests in just one young man and took the time to groom him and instill in him some of the knowledge that they were so fortunate to receive. *Each one, teach one right?* Or something like that.

Why do I come across the way I do? Maybe it is because I am that young man who needs grooming. One who is around affluent, professional black men on a daily basis but yet fails to make any real connections. I don't want the fish, but I damn sure would like to know how to catch them. Hell, maybe you should even lend me one of your old rods. Too much to ask?

I don't know. But one thing that I do know is, regardless of what your situation may be, the only chance you stand to make a way out of no way is through perseverance. Once I realized that the worst thing that people could say to me is tell me "No," I stopped placing limitations on myself and how far I could go. I've always had a small fear of rejection and as black men, we have this sense of pride in us that restricts most of us from asking for help for fear of seeming less than or weak. But when you put things in perspective, if your pride limits you from asking for help to make a better situation for yourself, *where's the strength in that?* As young men, we get so caught up and preoccupied in our personas and how we look compared to the next man that we lose sight on what's important. It is this crab-in-a-barrel mentality that got us all fucked up. And it's this mentality that cripples our supposed mentors and role models from being the light at the end of our misguided tunnels.

Whatever the case may be for you, never allow your current situation (NOW) to define your later expectation (FUTURE.) And I say "expectation" because you should expect to succeed, whether it is sooner or later. You may have to alter your dream, or carve a new path for your life, but your mindset, along with the hard work that you put in, should be that "IT IS COMING."

I don't know, maybe I'm trippin'…maybe I'm exaggerating. Whether or not these words will ever reach their intended millions, I'm not sure, but I would be willing to bet money that they resonate with a few, if not but just one. Take it how you want or don't take it at all, but this is how I feel. Hell it's all good anyway, I'm just talkin' my shit, remember?

6
P.O.B.

I'm a part of the generation that waits until the bestseller is sent to the theatres before I even try to read the story. I can't say I would be angry if this were sent to the theatres though. That would be THE GROOVE. Lol.

I have a lot on my mind, but I told myself that I would keep it to a minimum and stick to the point and task at hand. And that is making sure you understand my frustrations and possibly give somebody some encouragement to know that they aren't the only ones "goin' through it."

This is more than likely going to be the last chapter. After I write about men and women, I feel that it'll be time for me to exit stage left.

I entitled this chapter P.O.B., fittingly an acronym. It stands for: Perpetuation. Of. Bullshit. Webster's Dictionary and other sources define the word perpetuation or perpetuate as *"to make perpetual or cause to last indefinitely; cause to continue to be remembered; preserve from oblivion."*

And, in one way or another, we all know what bull-shit is.

I thought I would start here because when speaking on the topic of male/female relationships, I can get a tad longwinded. This seems to be the premise behind the majority of my "counseling sessions" and random conversation with people. I've been told that I give pretty good advice and when I go on my rants via Twitter and Facebook, I see now that I've established a small audience. Listen up, please.

What can I add in this chapter that hasn't already been discussed? I mean, we all know "niggas ain't shit." And about a few months ago, we found out that "these hoes be winning. I could go on and on with these lines that have us subconsciously sold on the idea that it is futile to think that we can have healthy rela-tionships as young people. I mean, hell, it's all we see and say! I could log on to Twitter RIGHT NOW, or Instagram, and see a Twitgram or tweet filled with some recycled ass line about relationships or men and women.

So, as I sat to think about how I would attack this last chapter, I came up with something. I would just stick to the script. I mean this whole book has been about us as individuals. I've given you a great deal of my life story and filled you in on the a few details of my current and former struggles. I've vented, been transparent, given you my heart on a platter like a Drake song, and just let you see me. The *real* me. I've given you my REALITY.

And this is what I choose to discuss now. REALITY. The reality that is US as people. To me, the word "reality" is really synonymous with the word "truth." When one deals with the reality of life, many things that cause uncertainty become defined. When dealing with reality, clouds of gray often times vanish into clear black and white definitions mixed with a little color here and there. What does this mean? Whatever your ideals, thoughts, hopes, dreams, and ambitions about a situation may be, if you are unable to assess and see the situation for what it is, you're fooling yourself. Ok, let me break it down even more.

How many of us watch reality TV? Okay, damn near everybody. Cool. Let's be honest; no matter if you're interest is in wildlife/hunting or catching great deals, there is a reality TV show for almost anything nowadays. Among my peers, the reality shows that are frequently talked about the most are ones that include "housewives of this" and "basketball wives of that". These shows that we have grown to love and adore give us an inside look into the lives of "celebrities" and their significant others.

What bothers me so much about these "reality" shows is the irony in the fact that they are truly *not* reality. Yes, these are real people in real-life situations, and I'm not knocking the hustle whatsoever, but I must do some damage control here. These shows have brainwashed us into really believing that the constructs displayed on these shows reflect an entire mass of people or an entire culture. Case and point: If you have ever watched "Jersey Shore" and knew absolutely nothing about that area, you would draw some really harsh conclusions based on the characters and behavior displayed on the show. Shit, I know I did.

We all cast judgment in some way, shape or form on people and more so if these people are our only or first impressions. Don't ever doubt that. So when it comes to reality TV, as it applies to my generation, the bullshit has reached an all-time high. First off, the majority of these shows depict these women as classy, wealthy, independent women who were all loyal to their men and ultimately get played only to find themselves struggling to pick up the pieces and move on. Boohoo. Sad story. Throw in a side hoe that has slept with their former beaus, backstabbing, pillow talk, and bottle-throwing and there you have these shows in a nutshell.

Now while these shows can be pure entertainment and fun as hell to watch while commentating on Twitter, the issue lies with the message that they are sending. Whether we believe it or not, mass media is slowly becoming this generations' reality. From social media to television and movies, we judge and guide our lives from the media's standpoint. If the Twitter community validates a concept or viewpoint as being "socially acceptable," guess what? That becomes the law. And when it comes to relationships, our society's over-sensationalizing of the dysfunctional black relationship has reached an all-time high, to the point where a majority of the traditional views on marriage and the family construct are so skewed, we don't know where to begin.

Reality. What is reality? To me, it is synonymous to truth. But one can also argue that perception is reality. And to go even further, that perception can equate what is true in one's life. Do you get where I'm going with this? I'm referring to a generation full of young people who are so easily swayed and led astray by entertainment and media that it becomes what defines our perception of the world and its various constructs. And so on and so forth.

No, I don't have a personal vendetta against "the establishment" or mass media in this society. Hell, I indulge in it on a daily basis. But at the same time, I am able to draw a fine line between the reality that is life and the reality that is shown to me via media channels. It is this reality that causes the issue for me. It is one that paints this absurdly, unattainable picture of perfect "dream" men and women in its movies and then turns around on the same canvas and draws another picture of trifling, emotionless leeches that it calls women and immature, irresponsible boys masquerading as men. It is these extremes of character traits that I find myself seeing exalted more often than not. Yes, now I truly understand what sensationalizing the negative has done to us as young, black people, hell, people in general. And while these extremes do exist, there is much more to us than that.

I explained a majority of what makes me the man that I am today. And a majority of my issues began at an early age. While I grew up surrounded by playboys and hung with young playas and pimps, my transgressions in the arena of love were always overshadowed by theirs. What I'm saying is, we all messed around, had a multitude of "chicks on the side," and "got it in" whenever we had a chance, but I was actually the good one. Although we did this all while maintaining relationships, as I've mentioned before, we all know that old habits die hard. And in my case, they die hard as hell. Now that I'm older, and am able to confront these issues with my significant others as I've had to over the years, I have noticed something so disturbing about myself and my friends. We have subconsciously rationalized our reckless, heartless behavior over the years the same way we did when we were young boys. Because I was always known as the one who "knew better" and had "the most sense out of the group," I internalized this by seeing my actions as always not being so bad. Why? *Because I know better! And I really don't mean to do what I do, it just happens, baby. I just need to get this out of my system.* Yep, I know my ladies are just shaking their pretty little heads right now, but hear me out. What my ladies, especially my sisters, usually fail to understand is that this is just as much of a cultural issue as it is about us as individuals. The same culture that affects what you wear, what you listen to, what is taboo and what's the "cool" thing to do is the reason why we just can't seem to get it right, ladies. I come from a single-parent home and didn't have many examples of healthy, monogamous relationships in my life while growing up. (No I'm not using this as a cop-out or an excuse, just try and hear me out.) The concept of monogamy is something that was more of a fairy tale than a reality to me. And the scary thing is that even while having a girlfriend, I never judged how good of a boyfriend I was to her by how faithful I was to her. Cheating was, and is, a way of life for us. And the older I get, the reality of this ideology that we as black men have instilled in ourselves, our sons and in society, is beginning to scare me. The reality that I am my father's son, a man with four children from three different women, and that I have his ways and have inherited his traits is one of the most horrifying things for me to deal with as a man. But we raise our sons to believe that the more women you have, the more power you have and the more of "a man" you are. How many black fathers do you know telling their sons that it is okay to save their virginity for marriage, whereas our daughters better have that thing shut down and on lock and key until the wedding night! So, you may have a young man, like myself, who knows better, knows how to treat a woman and what she deserves but still falls victim to a culture that has been imprinted on my psyche and my soul my entire life. The struggle is real. *Where and when does it end fellas?* Because what you see now, is ladies that have peeped game and have turned themselves into more refined versions of us. So whatever dirt you think you may be getting away with, our women are 10 steps ahead of us with alibis and evidence to prove. And thus, the cycle continues.

My shortcomings in the arena of love and relationships have hindered me but at the same time, have been needed to bring about growth and change. I acknowledge all of my fuck-ups. I know that I can't get any get-out-of-jail-free cards at this point in my life. And it took some serious soul-searching for me to make a conscious decision to mature and make a change for the better as a man. I'm not perfect by any means but willing to acknowledge that change is necessary. But now my question is, *will "she" accept that?*

Will she be able to take me as I am? The good and the bad? Will she believe that I'm worth sticking with through thick and thin to one day be able to love her the way she deserves? Because the media has told her that she deserves the best of the best of the best, sir, and I'm not going to argue with that. But since when did God begin to make perfect people? Maybe it was after I was born. Because that seems to be what we're looking for in this world. It is the perception that men are supposed to come as this big, bundle of love, under-standing and the big M word, MONOGAMY, that bothers me. Baby, it's not that simple. Yes, he may have it together financially, but sweetie you may still be dealing with a 16-year-old's mentality. As men, we don't engage our peers enough in the art of growing the fuck up. So, please believe that there are grown-ass men out here who think that they can have Plan A & B and see absolutely nothing wrong with it. (See Stevie J, "Love and Hip Hop Atlanta")

As much as black men try and dumb down their emotions and describe what makes us tick to be as simple as A-B-C, guess what? P.O.B. While we oftentimes refuse to tell you what is going on with us internally, please believe that it is the polar opposite. Between worrying about making enough money to compete with his peers, being the cornerstone of the family, and dealing with women, that can be a lot for any man. Let's not even throw in a child or two, paying bills for mama as well, emotional distress from an absent father (yes that is still an issue) and you have one big clusterfuck of emotion in an individual. As an aspiring psychologist, it is my view that black men and women are in the MOST need for counseling. So with that being said, why do we, in turn, look for each other to have it the most together?

Perception vs. Reality. As a young generation, we have to begin to draw lines between what we're fed and what we perceive as real. Sometimes it takes for you to go through some things (i.e. heartbreaks, breakups) for you to realize the simplicity in all of this. And for me, it is as simple as this.

You gotta get butt booty naked. #nosex

What the hell am I talking 'bout? I'm gonna tell you, chill. What I mean, is that when we begin these relationships, most of us rarely present our real selves. I know I'm guilty of that. I call them filters, just like Instagram.

Now some of us use more than others, but you got all these damn filters on the picture that is the real you. And just like Instagram, what happens? The more filters that you begin to take off, one starts to see you for the person that you *really* are and not the one you portray. And more times than not, this person doesn't like what they see. You base an entire relationship off of a filtered picture when you should've just handed them your scrapbook and let them decide if they liked the real you or not #nofilter. We don't fall in love with people anymore; we fall in love with ideas and perception. Because when all the filters are taken off, that is when the issues begin. When we're taken off the pedestals and seen for whom and what we truly are, that is when it becomes no-holds barred. That is when we deal with the aforementioned extremes. At this point, the concept of real relationships, in our community, start to become null and void.

I won't even say it takes time to get to know a person; it's more like effort. Actually try. Go a little deeper than what you're fed and learn the person who you choose to invest in. It takes *so* much to build a real relationship. Not these fairy tale romances that we've begun to believe are the norm. *The shit is hard!* This is

why, in a generation that thrives off of instant gratification, we too often settle for these filters and are ultimately left disappointed.

Reality.

Man, I'm just tired of the rhetoric, the back and
forth. I always catch myself like, "Can y'all just stfu
please?!?!" Stop complaining about what you refuse to
change. Either you invoke change or you learn how to
accept your mess and be happy. When will we learn
that everything doesn't come easy? Yes, love is patient,
kind and understanding. But *people* aren't. If you put
your imperfections into perspective, your ability to see
the next man will become 20/20. And when we begin to
expect people to be people and not God, we will be
much better off in the arena of love…and life.

I'm just tired of the same old BS. Tired of the rocks
being thrown from glass houses. Tired of the constant
extremes and the crazy expectations. Tired of the
negative sensationalizing of the black relationship. I
just want to challenge us as young men and women to
challenge each other TO BE BETTER. Not to be *perfect*.
Just to be better than you were the day before. Better for
each other, for ourselves, for our unborn children. Let's
start to single out these inadequacies, and instead of

using them to tear one another down, let us instead be the advocate for change in each other's lives. Because we need each other whether we believe it or not. Deal with the real, assess and grow. But please, let's stop perpetuating the bullshit.

7

On My Own
(Rap It Up)

"Ain't no nigga did nothin' for me, so I did it on my own..."

Here we are. One whole year later. I'm 24 now and as this book has shown, life happens. I've been through so many things in this year alone that I can't help but look back on it and thank God. The irony in the timing of me writing this final chapter right now is that my current situation is so different but yet so similar to how my situation was when I began writing this book. The maturity and progress in my faith in the Lord has overwhelmed even me at times, because God knows the amount of BS that I've been through in this year alone. I'm a believer that the true measure of a man is how he acts when he has absolutely nothing to lose and self-gratification is justified. *What do you do when you telling everybody to fuck off seems to be the only logical thing to do?* Lol. One thing that I can say, that I say almost every morning whenever I get on Twitter, is thank God for provision, protection and most importantly, progress.

This progress that has taken place in my life has left me so grateful for all the experiences that I've encountered. Whether good or bad, I learn and embrace everything that has happened to me and all that is currently happening. I say that this time in my life reminds me of how I was when I first began the book for several reasons. When I went back to look over what I wrote in the first chapter, there was one thing that stuck out to me while perusing my words: DESPERATION. Not desperation in a bad way, but reading those words brought me back to a time when my living room was nothing but me and these two green couches, a laptop, and my thoughts. It brought me back to a time where my fear of failure was backed by my firm belief that the Lord didn't bring me this far just to leave me now. As I sit here now and write this final chapter, tears rise to my eyes as I think about how far God has brought me from whence I came. You see, when you come from nothing, like my boy Kirko said, anything is coming up. I appreciate it all.

Cable. Internet. A damn iPhone! Lol. Now don't get me wrong, I've been on a rollercoaster ride from that time until now, but every time I'm faced with obstacles, I think right back to that first chapter. I think back to the time I was driving around Huntsville crying my eyes out because for the first time in my life, I was down to nothing. I think about what it meant for me to fight, scrape and claw my way up out of that financial hole. You're probably thinking that this is when I tell you my success story. Well you're right and you're wrong. My success is in the fact that I didn't let that shit beat me. I didn't make excuses for myself or my situation and I made a way out. I did not let my situation define me, and although my reality told me that I was on the road to failure, my perception of my situation was only that this was merely a stop sign on my road to success.

Almost every day I flood my social networks with words of encouragement, advice and insight into how I see my world and the various issues that we face. Daily, I'm received with love by people that see me as having it all together. Little do they know about me, and very few would probably say that I lacked for anything. Perception is a motherfucker, ain't it? King

Without A Crown. King. That I am. A motherfucking king and don't you dare think otherwise. I am God's Gift, the son to Misi, brother to Ehi, associate to many and friend to few. I carry myself with the demeanor of a man with purpose, and each day I attack this world with the knowledge that whatever problem I came into the day with, the blessing lies in the ability to be able to overcome it. My problems are like weights, as they pile on and I'm able to get 'em up off me; the stronger I become, the more "weight" I'm able to lift. Are you still looking for that success story? Well you're reading it. You're reading the very thing that will bring me up out of my current situation. You're reading a living testimony and I'm happy to share this moment with you. You see my purpose and intent of writing this book has become clear to me as the time passes. This book's intent was not for me to "vent." This book's intent was for you to see yourself through me. It was for you to understand that no matter how crazy your situation, it's effect on you is only as impactful as you make it.

I realize that this book may be a real look into my mind by those who know and love me the most. Well if you're reading this, know that I hurt, too. Know that my seemingly unshakable calm and reserve is really a front for the tsunami of emotions that I feel on a daily basis. Know that it takes everything in me to keep it all together at times when I want to be as petty as the people that I love the most. But I know better, so I do better. I know that God's plan for my life is to be an example and set a standard. Be an action, not a reaction.

The crazy thing about this book is that when I told some of my friends the idea behind it, I received heavy criticism. The fact that I haven't "arrived" yet, seems to be the reason this book WILL NOT sell. The fact that I'm "too southern" and "too street" will be the reason this book never makes it past Huntsville City Limits. Yes, maybe what I'm doing is something that hasn't ever been done but there's a first time for everything, right? I'm writing this book to tell you that you don't have to be limited by the vision others have. Your goals and dreams were given to you to manifest and not them for that very reason. When you're dealing with individuals whose vision is predicated on their provision, their lack thereof results in an inability to see further than their hands can touch. Oh ye of little faith. Yeah my approach is a tad Ochocincoish but I'll take his bank account over some of yours any day.

I believe in myself. I believe in this generation. The latter has been seen as absurd in the eyes of many of my peers and this fact bothers me to no end. We are so quick to say, "It is what it is." Naw, shawty; IT IS WHAT IT BECAME, and it can damn sure change. I refuse to succumb to stereotypes, and while my efforts to invoke change may not mirror those of Martin Luther King Jr., I pray that my passion for myself and my generation will show just as his did through my life work.

Tears and smiles. The conviction with which I write these words is so uplifting to me. The fact that I am at this point in my life leaves me speechless. You may not understand how it feels to reach the end of the road only to meet a bright, orange "CONSTRUCTION AHEAD: ROAD CLOSED" sign. You may not know how it feels when the plan you've made for yourself ends up being merely book notes to the plan God has for your life. As I said before, this reminds me of last year. Why? Because I'm down to my last. I'm back at a place where all I can do is look to the hills. I'm on the brink of a breakdown, teeter-tottering insanity yet still reaching for and expecting a blessing. But guess what? I smile. I smile because I have this. I have this ability to share my story with you and the ability to see my situation as I see the words in this book. Just another part of my story. If you're reading this, I thank you. Because it is for you that I wrote this and it is for you, my family and my God for whom I will continue to live. My time is now and this is just the beginning.

Sincerely and gratefully yours,

K.W.A.C.

Post Script

No, I'm not done. I have one last thing to say.

For those who read my book and are left with a myriad of questions, my job has been done. By no means is this book the end-all, be-all to my views and opinions on the many issues that our culture faces. I have encountered people who tell me that they need more, that they *require* more from me, and to these people I say, "In due time." Writing this book, in a sense, was like my first mixtape. Look at it as my demo to the world; all I am asking of you is to have open ears...and minds. I have never been one to stress quantity as much as I have quality. I will gladly take a music album with 10 great songs over one with 20 decent songs and only a few hits in between. This book was intended to leave an impact. Remember what it did for you, not how long it took you to read it. Remember what you felt when you read my words, not how much you paid to get it. This book was just me kicking down the door; kicking down the door of mediocrity in a culture that has become synonymous with the word, kicking down the door of apprehension and fear in my own life and kicking down a door that for so long, I feared would never open up. This book simply states to whom I choose to dedicate my life. I have come up with the term "generational activist," because that is then role I intend to fill. I intend to fight for us, all the while challenging us to do better. I intend to make a difference in the lives of my peers by forcing us to identify our imperfections, own up to our mistakes and not make excuses for our failures. I understand that the book begins at a particular place, takes you all around the world and then ends right back where it started. Yes, I know I gave you mere bits and pieces of some things. That was the point. The aim was for you, the reader, to get a sense of who I am. Maybe not the whole man, but a glimpse into what makes me Afu Okosun. This book's purpose is to motivate a generation of young men and women to begin thinking outside of the box and to stop limiting ourselves when it concerns how we define success. Men create culture; culture does not create men. We have created this machine that is our culture and in order for it to change, we must change. We must alter the way we think, the way we see the world, and the way we see ourselves. It is my firm belief that in order to move forward, one has to be able to sit still. Sit still and allow God to direct you in the way you should go. Too often we allow our **realities** to be controlled by our **fantasies**. By sitting still, you will start to see **your wants** becoming synonymous with **His will**. What I have realized in my 24 years of living is that I am as powerful as I allow myself to be. I use the term "allow" because so many of us are stuck on the corner, in the hood, on the field or in the studio and don't *allow* ourselves to be any bigger than that. We do not allow the gifts that we have been given to come to fruition and manifest in our lives because many times, they do not match up with our own expectations of ourselves. We do not own up to the responsibility of being our brother's (and sister's) keeper. And let's not even get started on how we treat the opposite sex. The irony behind these statements is that while we so strategically plan out the steps we take, our lives rarely ever end up exactly like the blueprints we strategized. So, what makes us feel that we truly know what's best? Yeah, I ask a lot of questions. The majority of them are hypothetical, but real all the same. It is only when we begin to ask these questions that we will begin to see a difference in ourselves that can evoke a real change. Simply put, the future is one scary mf. I don't know what it holds for me, but the one thing that I have come to terms with is that I will spend my life chasing my purpose and not a check. I read a quote that said, "People don't buy *what* you do, they buy *why* you do it." Authenticity is rare these days. Furthermore, in the quest for the almighty dollar, those who find the most success are those who are extremely passionate in their endeavors. I have learned this in my own life. No longer will I allow myself to just "get by." Satisfaction will come from knowing that my life was used to change someone else's. For me, that is invaluable. I pray that you enjoyed the book. I pray that it causes you to look at my life as an example for what accepting change and progress can and *will* do for you. Remember, this is just the beginning. But now, instead of just looking out the window, I hopped in the bucket, put my foot on the gas and got this show on the road. Be blessed.

Made in the USA
San Bernardino, CA
25 February 2014